TAKE OFF YOUR BRAVE
Poems Just for You

Words by Nadim (aged 4)

Pictures by Yasmeen Ismail

WALKER BOOKS
AND SUBSIDIARIES
LONDON · BOSTON · SYDNEY · AUCKLAND

A MESSAGE FROM KATE CLANCHY

The poems you're about to read are by four-year-old Nadim. This book got started because I worked with his mum, Yasmine – I'm a poetry teacher, and she wanted some ideas for teaching poetry to pre-school children.

I suggested a very simple idea: think of a real place where you put things down when you come home, make a list of them, then put down some feelings too. Yasmine decided to try out the idea on Nadim when he came home from nursery that day. She wrote down his every word and when he was finished, she read it back to him, sharing with him the sense that what he made was indeed a poem. This didn't only result in the writing of a lovely poem, but also helped Yasmine understand Nadim's feelings better.

After that, Nadim got quite into the habit of thinking up poems. When he went on a train ride, for example, he made a poem about what it was like. He made poems about his feelings towards school, and about family, and about learning to be alone, and about why people are bad. When I shared Nadim's poems on my Twitter account, thousands of people began to "like" them and leave comments like: "What a talent! What a poet Nadim will be when he grows up!"

And of course, he is talented. But he doesn't have to be a poet when he grows up.

Nadim's poems aren't special because they sound like grown-up poems – how boring that would be! – but because they sound like a four-year-old and tell us about his world. Nadim's special talent, his mum has always said, is being full of feelings and being able to share them. At the moment, those feelings are expressed as poems ... in the future, who knows? Maybe he will be a musician, a teacher, or a rocket scientist.

Now, Nadim's poems have been made into this beautiful book, where the pictures as well as the words are full of feelings. We hope that children reading this book with grown-ups will feel encouraged to make poems about their own feelings, so they can understand and share them better – just like Nadim.

Because poems aren't just for special people or special feelings. They're for everyone, about everything, and for every day. Try one.

Love

Everyone has to love someone
Flamingos loves someone
The wind loves someone
The sea loves someone
Spirits
Letters
Houses
Everything you ever know loves someone

Everyone has love
Even baddies

My Dream School

All the kids turn into kittens

      when they get into the dream school.

There will be no bullies

And the teachers are all friendly dinosaurs

And all they do is chat chat chat

      with anyone they want.

The school smells like daffodils, honey

And sometimes stinky socks.

(Some people faint when it smells like stinky socks.)

The kids are always making cardboard teleporters

But the grown-ups just sew toys.

Everyone loves that school.

Miss Angela

by Nadim and his sister Taleen,
written to their old nursery teacher

Miss Angela is nice.

Miss Angela smells like flowers.

Miss Angela smells warm.

Miss Angela sounds like a bell, ringing gently.

It makes me sad

that we're not going

to get to see

Miss Angela

every day

any more.

Bluebell, Where Did You Get Your Blue?

by Nadim's nursery class

Bluebell, where did you get your purple-y-blue?

Did you get your blue from the sea?

Did you get your purple from a purple butterfly?

Maybe the butterfly gave the bluebell a kiss?

Where did you get the green of your stem?

Did you get it from the grass?

Did you get it from a playset?

No, definitely not from a playset.

Did you get the green of your stem from a leaf?

And where did you get your bluebell smell?

Did you get it from the sunshine?

Did you eat the sunlight up?

You smell like blueberries. And glitter.

And butterflies fluttering around.

Being on a Train

Feels like *bumpity bump*

   Sounds like *chuka chuka shhhhh*

Smells a bit like air and eating smells

   Mostly sandwiches

It looks like being on a very giant long car

  But it goes a bit faster

    Goes to lots of cities and even countries

And is really bumpy

There's all these different stops

And stop stops are really different

Because it's like you're on a giant bus

  Because they're in the same country

In a train you think about anything really

      Sometimes you can think about it as floating

Or living in a monster's tummy

      Because it feels really moveable in a train

In a train you dream about anything really

      Like floating in a bubble in your home

          Sometimes you could be walking in a train

Looking for the time or your home or anything you want to see

      Like the moon

        Or a magic bus

My Best Friend

Eddie is not calm.
Eddie is fast.

He's as fast as anyone –
Faster than everyone –
Faster than anyone
And everyone you've ever seen.
And he knows pretty much everything
About aliens.

He lives near my old school in a house
(*it's made of bricks and it looks really cool*)
And it always has an orange flag outside
     And bikes
     And flowers
And there are always snacks at his house
And he shares his toys
(*they're really cool*)
And we play.

Tell Me About a Day of the Week

Wednesday is rainbow-coloured,
Because it's got all the colours in the world —
Because it's so lovely.

Wednesday's loveliness
Comes from the earth
And smells like roses.
And Wednesday wears a shirt with glitter on.

Tell Me a Lie About the Sea

The sea doesn't have any waves.
It doesn't make a sound.
The fish make the *shhhh* sound.
The seaweed doesn't have any names,
And it makes the *shhhh* sound too.

In the sea without sound,
The manatee finds its bed
In the coral reef
With the Nemo fish.
It snuggles up tight
In its beautiful coral bed and
Snugs to go to sleep. It's easy for it to fall asleep
In the sea without waves and sound.

Little
by Nadim's sister Taleen

This is a poem by my cute little pony. She's called "Little".

Because I've been reading,

learning, sleeping and eating.

And I've also been hugging and snuggling.

And I've also been loving my parents, my whole life.

And I've also been playing with my best friends.

And I've also been getting treats

like vitamin gummies and ice cream

and my things I wish for.

And I've also been exploring.

So I have learned so much,

during this holiday and in general.

Baddies

Baddies love their baddie friends
Even very baddie ones.

Nothing can make love disappear
Not spells
Not magic
Not mermaids
Not anything.

People might have rough moments
They might have sad moments
They might have shocked moments
They might have scared moments
They might have crackled moments
They might have unhappy moments
They might have really bad moments
But their love won't disappear.

Love in baddies

Love in good, protective people

Love in animals

Love in wind-storms

Love in penguins

Love in baddies, too.

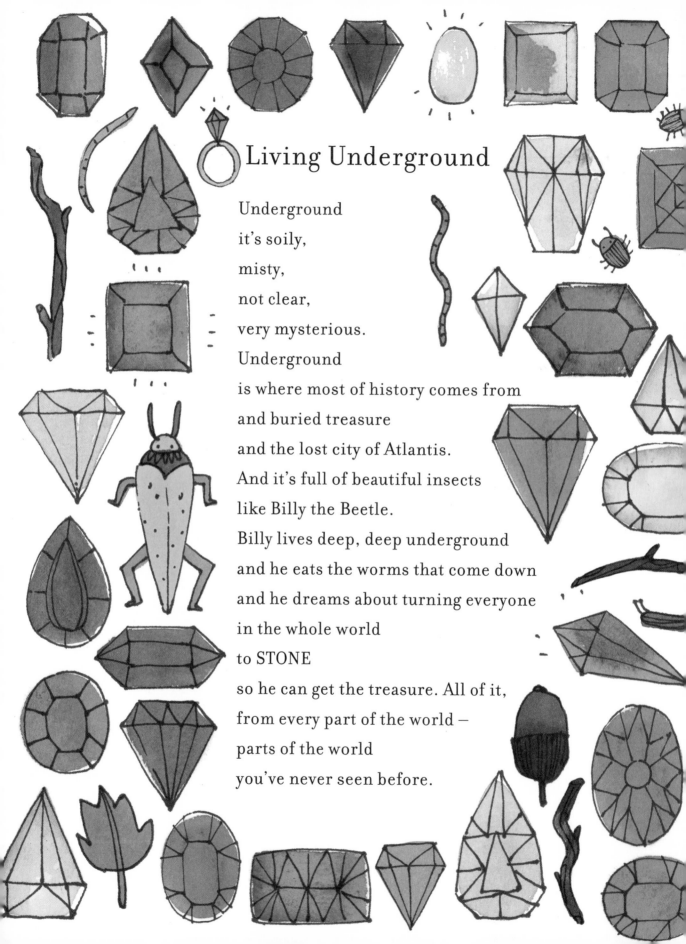

Living Underground

Underground
it's soily,
misty,
not clear,
very mysterious.
Underground
is where most of history comes from
and buried treasure
and the lost city of Atlantis.
And it's full of beautiful insects
like Billy the Beetle.
Billy lives deep, deep underground
and he eats the worms that come down
and he dreams about turning everyone
in the whole world
to STONE
so he can get the treasure. All of it,
from every part of the world —
parts of the world
you've never seen before.

The Busy Cat
by Nadim's nursery class

The busy cat wears ginger fur –
It wears a black fluffy hat.
The busy cat is eating lunch:
The busy cat eats tuna
And sometimes a salad with fish.
(The busy cat eats cat biscuits too.)
The busy cat waits for it to snow
So he can make snow-cat angels.

The busy cat smells like ginger —
It also smells like hope.
The busy cat hopes for a friend:
The busy cat's best friend will be a brave cat.
The busy cat's favourite time of day
    is naptime
When it puts on its sleeping cat
And it takes its little catnap.

Oh! My Best Things

Oh, owls!
Oh, playing with my sister, my whole family!
(Even if it's the whole big one
It's still my favourite.)

Watching William play football
   outside the garden window.
Playing with Daddy.
The smell of baked things.
I love love.
I love my family extra much.

Oh, glitter, Legos, books!
Looking at woodlice and bugs,
Eating ice cream
And snuggling
With you.

Memories

Sometimes, when I look at my memories
It makes me a bit sad –
Like when I'm at a different stage
It makes me think, "Oh…
I'm never going to get to do that again."

Mum, did you ever have that feeling?
Like when you went to school
And then it ended
And you started another one?

Magic Box

by Nadim

This box is for you, Auntie.

Covered in rainbow-glittered stars,

Filled up with lots of roses

And apples and oranges

So if you're hungry

You could just take one out

To snack on.

I'll put some secret toy elves in there

To play with, if you're bored –

They're electrical,

You can wind them up with a key in their back

That can make them talk or walk.

I'll put in the box

A baby moon

And pictures of smiley faces

That really smile.

I'll just close the lid

And wrap it

And send it with a magic spell

To you –

Even if you're just next to me,

Like right now.

Magic Box
by Nadim's sister Taleen

I'm going to send my magical box to Olivia.
I would put some magic pink stars in it
And Olivia will open them
And sparkly shiny things will glitter up.
I would send her a unicorn toy:
An Olivia toy.
(I wouldn't send my Unicorn
Who married Owly yesterday.)

I would send Olivia the moon.
I would send Olivia food.
I already sent her a lot of things –
And a hug.

My Lonely Garden

It's peaceful:

Calm.

Especially when

There are bugs flying around in the sun

And I get to just be thinking

On my nice blue bench

And all I can feel on my back is sunshine

And all I get to do is look at the beautiful plants and things

And do whatever I want

In my garden.

Moments

You always have sad moments

Happy moments

Nice moments

Angry moments

And when you smush those moments together

They make a great feeling

Called:

ABRACADABRACDOCUOUS.

For My Mum

Who was the one who feeds me mostly?
It's my mum, it's my mum.
Who's the one that baths me mostly?
It's my mum, it's my mum.
Who's the one who gives me snuggles?
It's my mum, it's my mum.

She's the one who does me airplane.
She's the one who takes me to Nursery.
She's the one who takes me from Lunch Club.
She's the one who goes to work in the world,
   for me.

You smell like a beautiful candle smell.
You smell like a candle when it blows away.
It smells really nice – the burnt bit.
You smell like a blown candle.

Take Off Your Brave

Take off our jackets
Hang them up

Take our gloves off
Take our shoes off
Put them where
They're supposed to go

You take off your brave feeling

Because there's nothing
To be scared of in the house:
No dark caves no monsters
No witches no bees no howling sounds

You don't need your brave anymore

Wash your hands

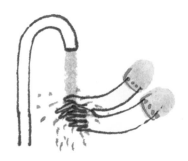

Eat lunch

Go get cosy.

Scared-Sugar

Did you ever have that feeling
That you were scared about doing something kind of scary,
But it was also kind of sweet?
Like the first time you meet new friends
Like touching a sea anemone
Like sleeping over at your cousin's house
Like eating a new food
Like becoming 5 instead of 4
Like saying bye to your mum
When you go to a new school.

You would feel nervous but excited
And that's a feeling called scared-sugar.

For scared-sugar things, you put on your brave
And you can take it off again, when you realize it's OK.
And that's it. Scary and sweet. Scared-sugar.

Between Bathtime and Bedtime

Can you get muscles in your muscles?

What does a cloud feel like?

What are all the fishes' names?

And what are all the animals called?

How much types of leopards are there?

What are all the names in the world?

Can you get muscles in your lungs?

Does everyone know what the moon feels like?

What do fire ants taste like?

How much types of gadgets are there?

What are all the parts of your body for?

What are birthmarks for?

How do they appear?

Is there any man on the moon?

Why are roosters important?

Does anything eat humans?

How did the world appear?

Is God actually real?

How much stars are there in the world?

Everyone loves poems.

How are bubbles made?

How do lightbulbs get their light?

I know that all of these questions are real

And poems are too.

My Wish

Was that we lived on a different planet
That was calm and quiet
With no countries or cities
Just a whole big town
That wasn't so busy
With lots of cafes and shops
And everyone was magical
Because whenever they moved their fingers
And said something they really wanted to happen
It would just come true very quickly

And on that planet

There were no deep craters

And there were beautiful flowers in all the seasons

Even winter

And lots of friendly and nice beautiful birds

And lots of them are robins

And lots of beautiful beaches

With lots of pearls and seashells

And lots of warm weather on the planet.

And lots of love.

And …

THE END.

For my Mom – N.

With love for Alasdair, Ted and Mystery Baby no.02 – Y.I.

First published 2021 by Walker Books Ltd
87 Vauxhall Walk, London SE11 5HJ

2 4 6 8 10 9 7 5 3 1

Text © 2021 Nadim Shamma-Sourgen
Illustrations © 2021 Yasmeen Ismail

The right of Nadim Shamma-Sourgen and Yasmeen Ismail to be identified as
author and illustrator respectively of this work has been asserted by
them in accordance with the Copyright, Designs and Patents Act 1988

This book has been typeset in Filosofia

Printed in Italy by L.E.G.O. S.p.A.

British Library Cataloguing in Publication Data: a catalogue record
for this book is available from the British Library

ISBN 978-1-4063-9970-7

www.walker.co.uk